four testimonies

*f*our testimonies

poems

KATE DANIELS

Louisiana State University Press

Baton Rouge   1998

07 06 05 04 03 02 01 00 99 98   5 4 3 2 1

Designer: Michele Myatt Quinn
Typeface: AGaramond
Printer and binder: Thomson-Shore, Inc.

Daniels, Kate, 1953–
    Four testimonies : poems / Kate Daniels.
        p.   cm.
    ISBN 0-8071-2259-9 (cloth : alk. paper). —ISBN 0-8071-2260-2
(pbk. : alk. paper)
    1. Women—Poetry.   I. Title.
PS3554.A5636F68   1998
811'.54—dc21   97-48849
                                                                CIP

The following poems first appeared in various publications, and are reprinted here with thanks:
Literary Quarterly (Oxford, U.K.), summer 1993: portions of "The Testimony of Simone Weil";
Five Points, fall 1998: "Genesis 1:28," "Moving"; *Image,* spring 1996: "After Reading Reznikoff,"
"Inscrutable"; *Louisiana Literature,* winter 1996: "Prayer for My Children"; *Southern Review,*
fall 1997: "Catholic," "Disjunction," "Funk."

The paper in this book meets the guidelines for permanence and durability of the Committee on
Production Guidelines for Book Longevity of the Council on Library Resources. ∞

for Geoffrey

Contents

The Testimony of Simone Weil

God can only be present in creation under the form of absence.

It is when from the innermost depths of our being we need a sound which does mean something—when we cry out for an answer and it is not given us—it is then that we touch the silence of God.

To love truth signifies to endure the void, and consequently to accept death. Truth is on the side of death. To love truth with all one's soul is something that cannot be done without a wrenching.
—*Simone Weil*

As Atget grew older, he made his pictures out of less and less. In his last years he seemed often to make them out of almost nothing.
—*John Szarkowski on Eugène Atget*

Other people do not know what to photograph.   —*Eugène Atget*

An Introductory Note

Simone Weil (1909–1943), the radical French political thinker and religious philosopher, was born in Paris, educated at the famous École Normale Supérieure, and worked as a teacher, factory worker, field hand, and political organizer before her death from self-starvation in England, at the age of thirty-four, during the Nazi occupation of France. Born a Jew, she embraced Catholicism, and has become as well known for her writing on supernatural religious beliefs and practices as she is for her left-wing social and political thought. Weil is perhaps best known for her final work, *The Need for Roots,* in which she addresses the physical and spiritual uprootedness of the modern world. She never married, but remained close to her mother, father, and only brother. A lifelong sufferer from anorexia, Weil also endured migraine headaches and many other minor health problems, yet despite these constraints, she completed in her short life a body of work that, posthumously published, garnered international attention and respect. She is considered one of the most prescient sociopolitical thinkers of the second half of the twentieth century. Her eccentric lifestyle (she routinely abandoned her comfortable existence as a teacher and intellectual to live and work among the lower classes), her anorexia, and her testimony on mysticism have all contributed to the ongoing interest in her.

Eugène Atget (1856–1927) made thousands of images during his career as an early documentary photographer, recording the visual remains of Old Paris and the emergence of the modern city. He began by producing photographic studies for painters, but soon broadened his interests. In the wake of Baron Georges Haussmann's modernization of Paris (which necessitated the destruction of large parts of the medieval city), demand arose for the preservation of what was left of Vieux Paris. Atget, whose photographs were purchased by supporting institutions like Bibliothèque Nationale and Musée Carnavalet, contributed more than four thousand glass-plate negatives to the effort. His style is noted for its elegant austerity, the eerie absence of human subjects, and extraordinary technical effects. In particular, he experimented with extreme lighting conditions, shooting directly into the sun to produce highly expressive flarings that appear as voided or burned areas on the image. Toward the end of his life especially, he often crossed the line dividing utilitarian documentation and the aesthetic concerns of art. He would have denied this, however, insisting until his death that his work consisted of nothing more than "documents."

There is no evidence that Simone Weil and Eugène Atget ever met.

I was born in Atget's Paris,
city of smoke and shadow and mysterious light,
the aristocracy's last-gasp sough of luxury and art.
Les misérables were invisible in that city.
Did they live there? Did anyone
live there but the solipsistic statuary
in the deserted wood?
The cart ruts in the park
proved someone had passed by—
or some*thing*—a wagon pulled
by an ownerless horse . . . but Atget's

       Paris

operated according to its own laws.
The buildings were its citizens, the landscaped parks
and stone-bound bridges its bourgeois children.
And the people who lived there?
They dissimulated themselves
for the higher purposes of the old man's camera—
a subtle smear of human dissonance
smudging one shot, a pantalooned leg amputated
by the frame in another.
They did this—or they disappeared
into Atget's images, trapped
by the flat, still walls of his inhuman vision.

I saw him once, I think, photographing
the Place de la Concorde. His wooden tripod
was propped in place by paving stones that had broken
from the curb. His bulky glass-frame camera in a box, huge

5

and cyclopic, was balanced atop like a monstrous head.
In the weak, wet breeze of January,
the black drape fluttered on his bent-down back.
His head was hidden but his arms screamed out
from the sides of the curtain, clearing the space
he intended to capture.

                                    People shoved each other
to the sides of the square until a curious emptiness—
a deep, still hole of angles and light—completely split
the afternoon in two
                                    and Atget shot.
When he signaled again, we surged back to the heart
of the picture Atget had never taken.
Standing there, unphotographed, my image not
captured on the glass plate darkening
with the cold, still shot, I sudddenly
imagined myself as Atget must:
a silvery dot of subtle movement, a grayish whirl
of churned-up air disturbed for a moment by bodily presence.
I saw, then, that we were nothing—or *thought*
we were nothing—that we would edit ourselves
out of the picture in favor of art.

*

In my own house, Papa had assembled
a vast galaxy of objects for our pleasure
and comfort. *Monsieur le docteur* made a prosperous
life. I laid my head on hand-embroidered
linen sheets at night. I hung
a little muff of pure white fur around
my neck. It warmed my hands in the Paris snow.
The delicate *tink tink* of old silver on the afternoon Limoges
was the first melody I knew. I think I tried
to recreate it on the pianola in the breakfast room.
In my father's library, thousands of books
on mahogany shelves. The unadulterated history

of the Western world, the gods and goddesses circling
Parnassus, the cruel facts of illustrated science
colored by hand in subtle tints. I installed
myself at the secretary, drop-front and *bombé*
with a tulipwood veneer—to contemplate the objects
that occupied that room: a crackled glass vase by Émile Gallé
given my parents as a wedding gift, a cigarette case
smuggled from Russia, allegedly designed by Carl Fabergé.
Beneath my hand, a coolly abstract paperweight: Baccarat.
And high in the ceiling, a gilt relief of four cupids
playing cards in the plaster cornice. These details somehow
                                        spoke
to me. Beauty, they said, was always a problem. Inevitably
purchased at a high price, devoid
of any function but giving pleasure,
it seemed immoral to possess so much
when others' lives were so impoverished—those disenfranchised
by Atget's images.
              "I do not like luxury," I announced at three,
and pulled the ribbons from my long dark hair,
divested myself of toys and games,
darkened my wardrobe to blacks and browns,
shapeless sacks that proclaimed my alienation
from aesthetic pleasure. The servants whispered
that I was a saint. Maman—more practical—despaired
of my severity, the frown lines deepening my tiny brow.
My life was a puzzle: a pimple raised to a hideous head,
oozing with comfort while others starved, were dressed
in rags, died for want of a hod of coal.

For awhile, it was a family joke: Simone the saint,
Saint Francis of Assisi recently relocated
to the Boulevard Saint-Michel in the body
of a young French girl. A Jew, no less. But then I took
to not eating. Instead, I worried.
The cook coaxed me with succulent bits
and Papa's hand found its way into my lap,
smearing my napkin with chocolate.

But I shoved my plate toward Maman
and asked her to give it to *les misérables*.

*

My first memory is of Maman—no: not of her
but of her breast, bursting with mother's milk.
Maman is sick. In her darkened room, the odors
are too strong, too sweet. She lies on her side
in the handcarved bed, unbuttoning, untying
her frilly chemise. "Give me the baby,"
she orders the maid, and then I am moving
through choking air, floating
to *ma mère*. She billows
the sheet above her breast, tenting me
in some *fin-de-siècle* modesty she can't
release even in illness. Her breast is huge,
pale pink and white, the veins swollen into dark relief
on the delicate skin. Thin crusts of dried milk
coat the nipple and then new milk is surging out,
sprinkling my face. Maman grumbles outside the tent:
"Quickly, Simone." And then
she plugs my mouth with it.

Perhaps it all began right there: buried
in my mother's bed, the breast offered
so churlishly and secretly.
                    The enigma of food was quite severe.
Not eating, I felt a deep pleasure in myself,
satisfied beyond any measure I had ever found.
My body diminished to a stark temple of delicate bones
tented by skin: inside, pure emptiness
and order, the architecture of Zen.
Periodically, I believed I could eat
                              nothing
and still live, fueled by the radiance of self-control.
                    Inevitably,

however, the weakness came, then headaches and fainting,
and I readdressed myself to food again.

But no one eats in Atget's Paris. In his *Bar de Cabaret*,
a wire rack of hard-boiled eggs stands complete.
No one is there. No one will be
there. It is over, or it's not begun—
either way, the eggs remain inviolable forever,
nurturing no one, growing nothing, hoarding their possibilities
for the grave of some garbage dump out back in the alley.
Somehow, it was always possible for me to eat eggs.
I liked them raw, in a drinking cup, whisked up
with a bit of sherry. Prepared that way,
it was like eating nothing, like drinking
the barest possible potion—an oily warmth
slid down almost before I could notice.
I got my menarche when I was twelve. Maman
described it in terms of eggs. In the library,
I found the sketch: the eggs clustered
to the sides of the womb. They hung there, like a cut
of grapes, suspended in a timeless moment,
awaiting the arrival of the spermatozoa. But my eggs
were like Atget's in the bar—destined
for no one, doomed
to grow nothing. They just sat there
in their ovarian racks dumbly acting out
the human race's guard against genocide.
For awhile, I used myself as an experiment
to study reproduction, but that was brief.
And then, no use at all for the monthly flow. I bore it
as I bore the impractical idiocies
of female dress, the suppressed
conventions of a daughter's life.

No secret I always yearned to be a boy, imagined
myself the second son, wore young men's
clothing—a tuxedo to the opera—

signed my letters home, Your son, Simon.
                                    In puberty,
however, I saw the folly of that. André
was the son: I, the daughter, forever trapped
by others' images of me, their
desires for me that I kept forgetting.
Despite Maman, I never learned
her womanly allure. Her dressing table was full
of silver and crystal mysteries shaped
into bottles—curious colors and exotic scents—
that made her irresistible to Papa
but never beckoned me.

He drove his hands inside the opulent bun
of her auburn hair one Easter night,
unleashing it on her naked back
while I watched, unobserved, in the boudoir mirror:
her undone camisole fluttering
from her shoulders like broken wings,
his body riding hers like Zeus' on Europa.
                                    Maman, Papa,
totally reduced to a state of matter—
no thought, no words but the keening cry
to the Christian god raised up into heaven.

Only once, I felt how that might have been—
my own strong nature surging up
like a bull restrained in a farmer's field
who senses the hole in a broken fence—
the brain gone ratlike and brutally beady, the body
a bulge of muscle and blood.
                              But I pulled myself
back. A red flag of warning
fluttered furiously inside and I heard
the voice of my teacher again, whispering in his insistent
cadence: *Descrivez exactement que vous voyez.*
So I did and suddenly

the storm was over. The cool, calm voice
of nouns and verbs had sorted it out, solved the equation
of passionate blood. The bull
fell dead, or trotted obediently back
to his trough, and I became
                              myself
again: a brain in a schoolgirl's uniform.

Unbidden, an image of the park at Versailles:
a whole row of marble busts
lopped off at the solar plexus
deposited atop man-high alabaster pedestals.

      Atget had photographed
      the one I loved, who seemed
      to be singing,
      precariously perched
      on his cold, hard post,
      mouth frozen
      in a tuneless *O.*
      An aria was still
      flooding through his head,
      perhaps, when he was captured
      this way—head tilted
      in an agony of pleasure,
      arms thrown back
      as he offered himself
      to the orgy of song.

And suddenly I realized
the orgy of pain could appear
identical: a saint
imagined in his final moments,
the lower half of his suffering body
burned away, the arms thrown back,
bleeding and roped to a sycamore stake.

*

In 1919, when I was ten, the Bolsheviks
completed their grand revolution,
smashing the palace, murdering
the family of Nicholas the czar.
At last, *les misérables* sat in state:
their wooden clogs muddying
the marble floors, their brats
caterwauling in the royal nursery.
"I am a Bolshevik," I told my friends.
The politics of deprivation flourished
in me—an antidote to the opulence
of my privileged life, it mitigated my guilt
at the ownership of property, the mindless diddling
with acquisitive pleasures *les bourgeois* loved.

                                        The left
loved *me*. Defector from the rich, brainy and articulate,
I imagined for them a perfect beauty
in working-class life, an harmonious balance
of body and brain, rough fingers sorting
the harvested grain, the natural clock of dawn to dusk,
the ascetic beauty of the worker's life—
no geegaws or technology impinging
on the course of nature, God's plan unfolding
as unproblematically as a mare foaling
in the new green grass of an alfalfa field.

As Atget longed to erase the poor,
I longed to erase *myself* to assume my rightful place
with those unnoticed in the margins of the world,
those rejected from the drawing rooms, ironing the lace
on a nobleman's collar for a few centimes.
So I repudiated my past to accomplish my work,
refute my fate as a privileged *femme*.
I would not marry, would not give birth.

Instead, I would think. *Je penserais.*
Ignore
            my body.
Become
            my brain.

*

Full of ego, I sometimes think
I evolved too soon—before the time
of real women, true
women, unsimpering,
unsentimental women.
I *was* a woman, wasn't I?
Regardless what the others thought.
                                        Inside,
full of tenderness as any
woman, soft at the core, turned
on the same lathe of negative
space, dark tunnel
tuned vulnerable, delicate
honeycomb, chambered but tough.
Yet no one *saw*
my woman, no one *felt*
my woman-ness, obscured
as it was by sensible dress, innate
and masculine clumsiness,
by *BRAINS.* They called me
"Martian," considered me in-
human, un-womanly. To be a woman—
the one they recognized—
was *so* absurd—hanging back
instead of plunging forward, denying strength,
keeping hands soft and gloved and clasped
in the lap, not staring
anyone in the face, not speaking, not
thinking, not being

anyone at all
who owns herself
but someone who always
belongs to others, anyone
at all who affords the price,
in the way that a portrait
of a beautiful woman—a naked woman—
belongs to the buyer. Painting purchased,
she's as good as dead
for what remains of the actual
creature who posed so proudly,
hair lustrous, body sleek,
rare thoughts churning in her living brain.

I couldn't *do* that because I *wasn't*
                              that:
a simpering construction of lace and idiocy
and personal liens.

I never belonged to anyone else.

*

Atget had an eye for whores.
He photographed them an entire spring,
dressed immodestly, hips
thrust out, corsets unfastened,
defiant faces blatant
with paint. They had lost
their *I*. Stripped to the center,
they devolved to nothingness
in the shape of a woman and her lingerie.

Outside a shop, in 1921, a whore posed,
smoking a cigarette in a worn-out petticoat.
The noon sun bore down, her shadow
scythed the street decisively

and purity blazed forth
from the frame. Atget
stopped in the street, the stones
clanging with his camera
put down, his breath hushed,
his eyes meeting hers, the smoky puff
of tobacco blurring the space
between them. The whole world rearranged
around her: Paris fell back

                    ashamed
of itself. It hung its head in the parlors.
It howled in the parks. The workplace
shuddered in realization but kept on going
anyway. And the whore smoked calmly in the morning cool.

Atget picked his camera up.
You look like a goddess, leaning there,
he might have said. *Your arms pale,*
your face chiseled with ancient emotions,
the weight of understanding nailing you
to the earth. And she, fingering the dirty ribbons
on her tattered chemise, she would have said,
Old man, it will cost you fifteen francs
to make my picture.

In his chest, Atget's heart seared
then froze. He shot the picture.
He gave the whore her fifteen francs.
Undone by his vision, heavily he bore
his instruments home. He would not weep, he would not
curse God. Instead, he would sleep.

He would sleep.

He would sleep.

*

Factory Work 1934

This world is prose. No poetry here. No verse. No lyric. No
lilt at the end of the line. No comforting surge to closure.

To test my ideas, I went to the factory. To verify my dream of
how it might be to immerse myself in the great hum of machin-
ery obedient to the hand of man. I found technology beguiling,
capable of making us larger than ourselves, stronger than we
were born to be.

But found instead the opposite. Not my utopia, but a shattered
colony of shattered individuals battling to stay minimally
conscious so their machines would not overtake them.

The power press
The metal-shearing machine
The stamping press

These were the machines I operated.

Or shall I say they operated me?

The man whose lungs were filled with lead
The man whose lungs were filled with blood
The woman whose brain was filled with blood
The woman whose husband expired on the line
The woman whose scalp was pulled from her head
The woman who brought her infant to work in a black valise
The child who died there, suffocated and alone
The man who glanced at the clock and lost his hand
The man who glanced at the clock and lost both his hands

And it was dead in there—walls reaching up thirty, forty feet,
the bland repetition of brick after brick, the lack of exit, the
absent vista, the mind roadblocked constantly, the eyes denied.

Identity Card A96630. That was me.

Alsthom Électrique, Forges de Basse-Indre, and Renault. Them.

My pay was 3 francs, 50 centimes per day. Enough for a roll,
a cut of sausage, a pot of coffee. The rest I spent on cigarettes.
How greedily I sucked the last one before punching in. We all
did. And then at the end of shift, rushing out to the vendors
waiting with their wood-wheeled carts to take our pay. Lighting
up right there. We might as well have disrobed in the middle of
the street. That's how intimate that tiny flame of comfort felt.

Have I mentioned the noise? The din of disunity, the unharmo-
nious tune of metal on metal. A metrical poem at top volume
gone bad and infinite. Imagine no deviation, no error, no
humanizing flourish of the individual imagination. Just that
marching music in metal. Stamping out 5,000 pieces of bow-
shaped brass each shift. In the factory. With no windows. Ten
hours straight at your personal machine. And then going home
through the streets of dark Paris with that noise in your ears,
that din in your head. Can't sleep it out, dine it out, drink it
out, bathe it out. Lying down with it there. Getting up with it
there and going back through the streets of still-dark Paris.
Going back *there* with *it there,* that damnable din still banging
in your head.

*

La politique de gauche

But Atget's vision never faltered in the lens; people
were *pentimenti* to him: *hats,* or *arms,* or a blurred
reflection in a glass, mute messengers from a painful
world he had banished from his documents. Still,
peeling back the surface of his austere and uninhabited
compositions, one might find the citizens Atget effaced,

invisibly enacting the daily motions of their lives.
That series, for instance, of *bourgeois* interiors
that Atget collected before the war—opulent
empty rooms testifying to superfluous
wealth, the lack of need, the absence
of soul. How he pushed the corners *in*
to reveal the human zero that resided
at the center. Pure vapidity
reigns in those rooms engorged
with their possessions—the glass-doored
armoire oozing with *objets d'art;*
the tapestries of *petit point;* the fringed
shades, the gilded glass, the swagged
drapery; the carved crown molding;
the marble statuary centered on the mantelpiece.

                    You can almost see
the owners of all this property belching
in the wake of a six-course meal, pushing back
from laden tables, uncorking the brandy, twiddling
the tassels of the maid's white smock. . . .
                    God comes
with his comforts to those
who need. And those who don't?
Atget found them here, inhabiting
these cold chambers, frozen in postures
of constant consumption, flickering
with the ghosts of godless gluttony.

*

Inventory

I have been asked
to make a list
of all I own:
I begin with my books,

my papers, my typewriting
machine. My spectacles,
thick and sensible.
My little room
I do not own—
bitter and dark
with cigarette smoke,
the old reek
of burned-up butts,
the sour pots of cold coffee.
The drapes I own, always
drawn, thick black crepe,
unlined and hung from rods
with nickel-headed pins
to block out light.
I own two dresses
and a coat, all black,
one pair each
of shoes and boots. Adequate
underthings, minimal
toiletries—nothing
more than soap and powder
for the cleaning of my teeth.
I often wonder
if I *own* my body
—if it's possible
to possess a God-created
thing—my wiry hair, large
nose, that mouth.

I own the scar
on my brash right
foot where I stepped
in a pot of heated oil
watching the war
in Andalusia. I own
my bad stomach, its finicky

tastes and poor pleasures,
its kinked-up bowels.
I own my empty mouth,
my not-eating,
my loose teeth and bleeding
gums. And finally, I own my sex,
that fragrant, celibate
garden I cultivate for God.
Not one of your picturesque
ruins everyone
points a camera at—
a rusting iron
gate in a château
wall, nor even the simpler
closed wooden doors
in a stone wall's circle.
But this modest wire mesh
on a wooden frame that Atget saw
in Châtillon, the complex forms
of a leafy tree's pruned-back limbs
twisted overhead in a gnarled bower.

How shall I enter,
on the list of all I own,
this vulgar gate and common
plot that lies beyond
that Atget found
the beauty in? Unseen,
unmown, it dominates
my life. I go there
to recline, facedown,
beneath the kidnaped
clouds of Atget's universe,
the sky, as usual,
eviscerated light,
rupturing absence.

*

Love

Decreation: To make something created pass into the uncreated.

We must become nothing, we must go down to the vegetative level; it is then that God becomes bread.   —Simone Weil

"You must sit down," says Love, "and taste my meat."
       So I did sit and eat.   —George Herbert

It must be this to love
someone, to *faire l'amour.*
To come upon that moment finally
and find it falling apart beneath one's body,
the whole world reduced to the size
of a bed, huge fissures quaking open,
garbage dumps for words and thought.
Terror that the mind has proceeded
as far as it can: shrunk down
to nothing, diminished to air.

Looking into His eyes at that one
unknowable moment when all colors gain
in vividness, sounds debride, and touch
is a new realm of knowing. The shining nail
is sunk in desire, and you burst through
a hot spurt of pain, then pleasure,
to the other side, mindless and mute,
where you never planned to be.

*

Technique

Because he points his lens into the sun,
the clouds have been burned away,
the sky scoured of all but glaring light.
And pressing up from underneath, foliage assumes

a violent thrust

of darkness in the center of the frame.

What was it Atget saw when he prepared this shot,
perspiring beneath the smothering drape,
fiddling endlessly with his ground glass lens
until he formed just *this* image, just *this*
expression of the Côte de la Concorde.

In my mind, it is here I live—a dark blurt,
a blot in an atmosphere of unrelieved
intensity, immanence of pure light boring
all humans into black relief, divesting us
of detail so we become worthless documents
in the gallery of art.

                    There we are, arising
from the metal tray of acid wash.
We didn't know we looked like that—
a man whose head is in fact a hat;
a woman so brittle she threatens
to tip from the frame of the shot; a wounded
statue; a kitten blurred
to a sodden ball of fur and paws; an un-
slept-in bed; a dead tree; a broken
pot; an empty square; an empty score of metal chairs
outside a closed and shuttered restaurant.

I live here, inside these fractured
voids, full of a yearning Atget photographed
as light bearing down with painful tenderness
on all that is broken and forgotten,
all that cries out for relief and for mercy.

*

Epiphany 1938

In a stone chapel, in the south of France,
I found God, the son of God, the unimagined man
of my dreams. There on my knees, on the damp cobbles,
head pounding as usual, I asked for once for nothing,
nothing at all, just opened myself completely, totalizing
into something like a clear glass goblet. No, not
closed off at the bottom like that, more like a funnel, a channel
that something might run through, charge through, sparking,
finally, my body into knowledge.

That I was poor and wretched I could not doubt.
That I was undeserving I knew with certainty.
That I understood nothing was confirmed for me at last.
That mercy was mine anyway, I realized, touched,
suddenly, as I was all over, scalp tingling,
spine rushing with hot fingers, heated needles, up and down.

In Atget's series of the ragpickers, *les chiffonniers,* garbage
is the harvest, trash the kingdom of those who would live
indentured to no one but the Lord. Ragpickers were the chosen
people of Eugène Atget, and in the Benedictine chapel at Solesmes,
I became the *chiffonnier* I had always been. The ancient, sculpted
stones might rear above me in the shape of majesty,
but I was someone small and new, that tattered child Atget caught
playing in a pile of rubbish with a sweet, unruffled kitten.
Or the one sucking her dirty thumb by the base of a tipped-over
cart—small comfort of a child prisoner of poverty.

And now I could complete my journey, enter, finally,
that image of the rue de Bievre with its marvelous eruption
of curling light. There, on the left, where Atget could not resist
the pile of wrecked carts, I will abandon, at last,
my feeble body, and step out onto that luminous
sheen of curdled light and feel no separation, no loss,

and take no step, make no move toward the vanishing point
at the end of the shot. I will stay so silent, so still,
I will almost hear Him coming.

Dialogue / Epilogue

The noise of shadows

in the mind

The weight of light

on the body

The interrogating document

of personal property

The formal rules of composition

in prayer and in poetry

The aesthetic desirability of distance

and remoteness from emotion

To invade a scene with artistic consciousness

an intuitive form of politics

To disappear the undesirable

a godless act

To take up the camera

an act of faith

To ask what lies on the other side

of these bodies we inhabit

If anything

these lives we live

Accepting one's vision

annihilates the self

IN THE MARVELOUS DIMENSION

―――――――――

Affliction is a marvel of divine technique. It is a simple and ingenious
device to introduce into the soul of a finite creature that immensity
of force, blind, brutal, and cold. The infinite distance which separates
God from the creature is concentrated into a point to transfix the cen-
tre of a soul. . . . In this marvellous dimension, without leaving the
time and place to which the body is bound, the soul can traverse the
whole of space and time and come into the actual presence of God.
—*Simone Weil*

(John)

Until then, I'd never liked
petunias, their heavy stems,
the peculiar spittooning sound
of their name. Now I loved
a petunia for all it was worth
—a purplish blue bloom
waving in a red clay pot outside
an office window. My right eye
could see it through the shattered
windshield. My left eye had gone
blank and the roof of the Camaro
pressed my head flat back on the seat.
I diminished to my right eye,
which could only see, past the wreckage,
that one little flower. I felt myself
growing smaller, like Alice,
a trick so I could travel
out of there, to that ledge
where a petunia waved in the dust rising
from a fallen-down freeway.

✝

(Mary)

I picked the kids up
at 4:45, as usual.
As usual, they were antsy
and fighting. Rose tore a hole
in her new knee socks
kicking Justin in the backseat.
Timmy sucked his thumb in the corner.
Then Justin wailed at another
abuse from Rose and I was just about

to yell, *Goddamnit, shut up for once,*
when the whole thing went. I mean
the whole thing, the whole world,
I thought. The car tilted, the road
buckled up and then something was falling
down on us with a horrible screaming.
I guess I stopped driving and turned
to my children with a face of horror.
I reached past the seatbelt for Timmy,
my baby, and that's when it hit us.
My hand, pressed by the roof, pinned
his leg to the seat and he screamed.
Blood flowed down. Rose, my sweet
little Rose, was already gone.
I couldn't find her beneath
the bulged-down roof. Justin and Timmy,
they looked to me. They didn't understand
I was not in charge. I'd always been
their only God. They looked to me.
They wanted me to lift them up
and wipe them clean, to mend
with tenderness their shattered bodies.
But I was pinned in place. Blood
started seeping from Justin's
mouth. Timmy never spoke again.
And then I knew everything: how we
were going to die and how it didn't
really matter in the scheme of things.
My babies' suffering wouldn't matter.
It was a board game of gigantic
proportions. Our tokens
had been shaken out on the playing board
at 5:04 P.M. on the 17th of October
in the year of our Lord, 1989.

(Jane)

I must have been unconscious.
Even now, I can't remember
anything about what happened
until that arm
reached in the broken window
of the passenger seat.
It was just an arm, a black
person's arm, very strong
looking with fine hairs
all over it. The fingers
moved on my face, felt
my mouth, and then I heard
a voice shouting, *Someone's
alive here, breathing.*
I knew then it was me.
I was alive but I must be
in trouble. My body
returned to me slowly.
I was laid out flat on my back.
The roof of the car seemed
to be on top of me.
I couldn't feel anything
but my face where the arm
had touched me. I couldn't help
thinking about sardines
in their little oily cans,
how, in college, I ate them
on saltines, to save money.

(John)

Years ago, on a lark,
I learned transcendental
meditation. Now I focused
on the blue petunia and slowed
my breathing as I began to understand,
I thought, what had happened.
The whole fucking thing fell down.
I can't begin to explain
that terror. I've put it
in a little box in my brain
and I'm afraid of the day
it will emerge again. That petunia
saved me. Now I have
a whole garden of them
and when I wake at night
with the shits and the sweats
I go out there and lie down
among them, blooming or not,
cold or hot, and I weep long
and deep into the earth.

✝

(Mary)

My baby was the last
one to go. *And the last
shall be first.* I hope
it's true. My children
dead around me, I couldn't
think of anything to do
but sing the lullabies I sang
when they were infants in their cradles
and I was sending them away
to oblivion for the night.

(Jane)

When I meet people
now, I look at their hands.
I know I'm looking for *that*
hand, *that* arm, the one
that told the world
I lived, that proclaimed me
worth saving. My own hands
lie on the arms of the metal
chair, useless and heavy.
One finger on each has enough
strength left to press these buttons,
moving me forward, moving me
back. I don't think
it would matter, anyway, to still have
the use of my body. It's only hands
I care about, my mouth that still
loves. Even in sleep, I feel
his fingers reading my terrified face,
tracing my lips like a patient lover.
He found my breath. You bastards
can have my body.

—⚊—

I couldn't believe it
when I heard this little voice
singing *We Are Three Little Lambs.*
I thought it had already
gotten to me, like in 'Nam,
when I freaked out
on patrol before anything
had happened. But the voice
was real, coming from a dark blue
Toyota squashed almost flat.

When I shone the flash over it,
I could see the dark pool of blood
beneath. In the dark, I could
smell it. I yelled out, *Ma'am—*
I'm here to help you, and the song
stopped for a moment. Then a voice,
not little at all, harder than any
I've ever heard, said from deep in the wreck,
You might as well go away. Nobody
can ever help me again.

✝

(Mary)

People have actually asked me
what I thought about in there,
if I figured I would get out,
if I knew the children were dead.
The answer is: when I knew
the children were dead, I didn't want
to get out, couldn't get out
anyway. I was in there
forever with my three little lambs,
the smell of their blood,
and their dead faces, filled with questions,
looking at me.

———

(John)

When I do die, give me nothing
but petunias. Pots and pots
of them with their unpretentious
blossoms and their lack of smell.

—⊸— † ↩—

(John, Mary, Jane)

It suddenly struck me
that I believed
the unbelievable.

†

(Mary)

The freeway had apparently
fallen down on top of us.
My children were dead
and dying. My head was locked
into position to watch that.
The only way to not see
was to close my eyes.
But my baby lived
a long time, I think.
I had to look at him
as long as he survived,
to say those things that mothers
say, *It's OK, Mama's here, it will be*
all right. All the while
I was not exactly remembering
my past, but feeling
the future. It had a shape now.
I knew what I was doing
and what I believed.
I was watching
all three of my children
die. More than ever
before I believed
in God. He was there
in that car. He caused

it, He saw it. And when
it was over, He'd gotten
what He wanted.
One more fearful
citizen bowed down
and kissed His feet.
And then, goddamnit,
I led my babies right up.
I put their little hands
in His, and delivered them over
for eternity to Him.

—⚬—

I was shaving at the sink
and drinking my second cup
of coffee when the story
about that woman and her three
dead children came on the news.
I'm a man, but I screamed
when I heard it, the saw
and all. How they had to
blindfold her, what they told her
they were doing. I'm a man
but I screamed about this world
men built.

†

(Mary)

I never went to college
but I know now there's something
more than this world we see.
Trapped in that car, I felt it
when Timmy, Rose, and Justin

expired. They just left, and for awhile
I went with them. We eased
right out of that wreck
and floated in a void
—a marvelous dimension—
like big flecks of ash
freed from a fire.
That's why it didn't matter
when they took their bodies.
They had left them already,
and were part of me again, as they were
to begin with, making me bigger.

(John)

I'm lucky, I guess.
That petunia got me
through it. I came out
with fear and a limp.
Not like that poor woman
who lost her kids or the quadriplegic
in the car near mine.
The magazines all want to know
what it's like, but who could describe
your whole world reduced
to the size of a washer,
your body twisted
around the spindle, fear
churning through, and nothing
to help but your brain. I was in there
for three hours and forty-eight
minutes, thinking clearly every second,
reckoning nonstop. Oh, yeah,
I prayed, and I believed. I *saw*
my life. It had a shape

at last and I wasn't ashamed.
I knew if I made it, I would worship
the planet, the natural
world, eschew concrete,
deny the cities. I would plant
petunias, groom evergreen trees. In short,
I would worship the earth,
not men.

✝

(Mary)

Their father came over
from the city for the funeral.
He was drunk and terrified
to look at me. I wasn't drunk
and I wasn't scared. People looked
at me like I was a monster—dry
eyed and calm. But if they'd
touched me, they would have known:
hard as metal on the outside, empty
as a suit of armor within.

ᴐ‍

(Jane)

The most intense feeling
I've ever had was that man
touching my face. Even now,
when I can get
someone to do it,
I almost swoon with the shivering,
the delicious sensation
ascending my face.
I'm being born

again, being pulled
from my mother.

And a second chance is offering
itself in the form
of a hand,
      a simple
          proffered
              human hand.

—⁂—

           I can't imagine
           going through that.
           Can you? Watching
           your own kids die.
           Or coming out paralyzed
           or soft in the head
           forever. Thank God
           it wasn't us. Life
           could never be the same,
           could it? How
           could you bear it? How
           could you live?

✝
(Mary)

I live somewhere else
now. With them. It's not
in space, not
in time. It's pure
feeling, spread out
like jelly on a warm piece
of bread, sinking down

out of sight, the sweetness
still there, sodden
and hidden.

◦‿

(Jane)

I used to look at cripples
and wonder how
they stood it.
I never could, I thought.
Now I thank God every
day I'm alive and a crip.
I laugh with pleasure
and get the nurse
to run her fingers
on my lip.

—ᴍ—

Those motherfucker newscasters
stood in front of the freeway
and broadcast their pithy little
stories every evening while people
were dying inside. Now *that's*
my definition of indecent.

✝
(Mary)

A preacher came to see me afterwards.
He asked me not to be
so angry, to forgive God,
to try to see it as part

of a plan I could not understand.
I just looked at him and he saw something
in my eyes that scared him: those three
little babies, frightened as bunnies. *I can't imagine
your pain,* he finally said. *I wouldn't try to.
Can your affliction bring you closer
to Christ? Can you be with Him
in your suffering?* And then I did something
I'll never regret: I laughed
in his face, I brayed like a donkey.

—⁂—

She just kept
weeping for her babies
and he was raving
on and on about some
flower in a pot. The paralyzed
one had a beautiful smile
on her beautiful face. I don't think
she could feel
a thing.

(Jane)

When they pulled me out,
my body was dead
already but it didn't
matter. I felt the best
I've ever felt. That one hand
gave me hope. Other hands
pulled me back
into life. I wouldn't let
myself begin to believe

41

until I saw the sky
again. Widening and
widening, it revealed itself
in the shape of a lip
curved up.

—∾—

           Like everyone else, I watched it
           on television for three straight days.
           There was nothing a person like me
           could do. The twentieth century
           caved in finally. The earth
           taught cement a permanent
           lesson. Now, it's not
           that I'm phobic. It's just
           that I've seen postmodern light.
           We're all insane
           to live this way.

           ?

           The earth settled.
           The waters calmed.
           The planet twirled
           in the heavens
           unconcernedly
           again.

✝

(Mary)

When the priest raises
the pale white Host

something really does
happen if you want
to believe. If you don't,
it might still happen
anyway. Right?
Your past wiped out
by the force of the mystery.
The future emerging
from one huge moment . . .

Once, at a student play
in seventh grade,
the whole backdrop collapsed
with the wheezy singing
of nails being forced
from cheap wood. Frayed ropes
dangling like live snakes
and sawdust rising in a smoky haze.
When the scene settled,
Reality was where
it had always been:
right *there,* lurking
behind the drapes:
a cinderblock wall
painted pale green and a red door
marked Emergency Exit chained shut.
For once, nothing
but an empty stage separated
me from It. I *was*
It, and It was this:
several million tons of concrete roadway
and steel beams smashed
down on top of
approximately 274 live human beings
when the San Andreas Fault flexed a tiny muscle.
39 died, including my children. I
survived. Hundreds

took part in the rescue effort.
The rest of you—Christ
have mercy—watched on TV.

—⚬⚬⚬— † ⚬⚬

(John, Mary, Jane)

The red door
was chained shut.
We went through it
anyway.

for Janet May

THE SMASH-UP

On the whole, our present situation more or less resembles that of a party of absolutely ignorant travelers who find themselves in a motor-car launched at full speed and driverless across broken country. When will the smash-up occur after which it will be possible to consider trying something new?   —Simone Weil

1.

Her husband took his life
last night, drove the car to a local
lovers lane, and there, all alone
in the humid darkness, made the gestures
that composed the end of his life.

She, too, was alone at that moment,
back home in the bedroom, lying
on the bed in the aftermath
of one last quarrel, cool moonlight
pouring in the window, the neckline
of her nightie wrenched out of shape.
Coolly, she studied her nails and calmed
her breathing, while his last breath
expelled in a splattering rush. What images
of her swept through his mind
at that moment? Or was it, as she once
suggested, all about *him,* his hairy fists hammering
a temporary image of himself on her cheekbones,
her nightgown ripping in a scenic tear
as she made her own set of futile gestures.

First, I see her in supplication, appealing
to his better self, and then, recognizing
how distant he is, how long it has been
since the two were one, she lies down
in front of him and simply gives up.
She pilots her mind to another shore
and rests there, calm, at the edge of the water,
until the storm has passed, a supine
Venus returning, in despair,
to the solitary deeps.

For me, her mother, to see her this way
is more, really, than I can bear. For a moment,

I envy *him,* safe in oblivion
forever, his mind cleared
of images for eternity,
memories dislodged and shaken
free in one loud moment,
a single gesture giving him
that freedom, while I still live,
remembering. . . .

2.

I suppose it matters little now to confess
I never liked him. Behind the curtain,
before the priest, I said it many times
and was counseled to acceptance. I hated
the way he touched her, as if she were
his grandest possession, hated, too, how
she glimmered at that touch. Once, I saw him
stroke her jawline with his middle finger, then drop
his hirsute hand to encircle her throat. The secret look
that passed between them made me ill,
chilled me in a way that filled me with the realization
I'd remember that day's gesture—a late fall afternoon,
drinking Chardonnay in the sunroom at my home,
the glassy sunlight breaking almost full
through the all but empty trees, the sky
that glowering, truculent blue that announces
the end of autumn has come. I asked myself then
what I had done to encourage this in her,
how I had helped her see herself as nothing more
than the agent of his pleasure. Her occupation,
I suddenly realized, was that of glamour—static,
time-limited, and narcissistic. Then the weather
broke suddenly, as it often does in late fall,
and I rose to shut a window. It clattered

in its track and latched automatically. Before me,
the vista changed its hue—periwinkle poured
down the sky, darkening my view.

3. *In Therapy*

Does anyone really lie
down on the couch? I can't
do it. It seems so
vulnerable, the soft parts
of my body laid out
like a steak on a slab
while he sits barricaded
behind a great oak desk
taking notes and asking
minimalizing questions.

Q. How did you feel
    about being pregnant?

A. Fine. I was happy
    about it. We planned it,
    you know.

> *But I loved being pregnant,*
> *a body tucked inside mine,*
> *ticking like a bomb, growing*
> *impossibly fast. At night*
> *I lay in the darkness*
> *beside my sleeping husband*
> *and imagined her sprouting hair,*
> *hardening nails, the glistening,*
> *oozy liquid of her eyeballs,*
> *the plump pink worm of her silent tongue,*
> *her sex ripening like a scarlet lily.*

Q. Is there anything else
   you'd like to tell me?

A. No.

> *How can I tell I gave birth*
> *to the universe, what a god*
> *I was, how omnipotent, how*
> *large. You stupid man,*
> *what can be said about making*
> *a creature, a living creature,*
> *from a homely, mortal body?*

Q. Are you sure?

A. Of course . . .

> *not.*

4. *Gravid*

Crazy with this
richness, flesh
ball of stomach, warm
hefts of breasts. My hair
becoming an auburn pelt. Groomed
by the universe, I
thrive, I thrive. Swollen
my sex and tender
my love, for above it
she hangs, sweet
fruit ripening, gift
of the goddess.

5. *Domestic Violence*

The first time
he hit her.

The siren of stitches
on her fine-boned cheek.
The continent-shaped
bruise on her taut
white thigh.

The wire coathanger
twisted out of shape
on the bedroom floor.

How they made love
afterwards, the blood
on the sheets.

The way she lay there
like a fish dynamited up
from the bottom of a pond,
stunned but temporarily
still alive.

6. *Mid-Life Feminism*

There was a moment I thought she might have transcended the
obscene cultural image of womanhood we maintain. She was
eleven, crazy about horses, brilliant at math. She wore her hair
in long, practical braids, tied off at the ends with colored rib-
bons. Her best friend was another girl just like her. They wrote
poems and mixed their own granola and calculated how long it
would take a girl like themselves to walk to the moon. They
believed anything was possible, still living in a world without

bras and menses and the regard of men. Then one day on the
school bus, an older boy, fifteen or sixteen, negated my daugh-
ter, my beautiful daughter, pronounced her "that ugly bitch"
who was blocking his view of some already adolescent girl-child
who squirmed and glimmered under his approving gaze. For the
first time, she was crushed. Then, her breasts started pressing
past her body, and her friend, horrified at her own changes,
stopped eating and ended up in the hospital with a tube surgi-
cally implanted in her solar plexus.

There followed some seasons of solitude. Her father left,
and I went to work full-time. The next time I remember really
seeing her, her hair was sliced up one side in a fashionable cut.
She wore short skirts and riding boots, a desperate gesture back,
perhaps, to her girlhood, when her feelings about her body
belonged to herself. Once, I found her mooning over a picture
of her favorite horse and that little girl who eventually died from
self-starvation. My heart broke belatedly. But by then, it was too
late. She had already been colonized by the culture, carved up
into tits and ass, required for nothing but her beautiful body.

7. *Divorce*

Climbing the stairs
at the back of the garden
a tipped nest testifies
to a broken household,
rich yolk erupting
from a shattered shell.

8. *Righteous*

Demeter is not
the Phoenix. Not
rising from the ashes
of her own tragedy. Not
forgiving.

Demeter refuses
to be shushed or appeased.
Will not settle
out of court, nor make the best
of a rotten situation.
Will not forgive.
She is pure rage
in dreadlocks and chipped
red nails, searching
searching, searching
for her girl.

She sucks a stone
to quell the moans rising
in her throat and all the world
subsides, falling back
into winter, stunned
by crisp frost and stripped
branches, the sky
like a broken lightbulb.

Brooding ruins all seasons,
doesn't it? Grief growing
like a tumor, a mother grieves
growing old alone, the telephone
silent on Saturday morning,
the once-neat nest gone cluttered
and dirty, in disarray.

As the line avoids the enclosing
circle, Demeter defies the holocaust
of fate. The straight line
forges her unique dark power—the arrow,
the gun, the battering
ram. It steals the world
for itself, fights fire
with fire. Demeter sits
on her nest on her eggs

of misery, sharpening
her senses. A whiff
of her girl wafts up
from the hell of some
all-men's world and she's gone,
racing. Certain
and righteous, haunches
taut, fur flying, nipples
contracted into hard
black bullets.

Demeter is not the Phoenix,
not Gandhi or King or Jesus Christ.
That man in the Baton Rouge airport
hiding himself in the telephone booth,
gun in hand, awaiting the transported prisoner,
the one who raped his third-grade son—
that's Demeter, neither woman nor man.
Raw mother—a tensed claw
in a pink silk glove.

9. *In Church*

Nothing for me here now
but another man and more
violence. Words rain
on my head, my hands.
Looking down, I see
my nails are bitten again,
red at the edges, cuticles
seeping blood. How
appropriate to leave blood
here, wiped into the tufted
cushions of the wooden
pew, and walk out
with clean hands,

an empty heart,
with nothing to believe in
but the hard facts of the broken body.

10. *Graveside*

All the times she didn't weep,
and now, here she is, crying
for that bastard. Her black tulle veil
sighing in and out to the ragged rhythm
of her quiet sobs. The pastor says
a few noncommittal words. The mourners
look embarrassed.
                        I won't
walk away before this is over, before
the monster who devoured my beautiful
daughter is lowered in the ground. I nod
at the workers. In the bright sun,
machinery starts up a calm thrum
and I stand and watch. He's going
down now, finally, into the cool
dark earth. Let him think about it
                        a long time. Let him suffer. Let the creatures
of the earth lay their hands on him
in an unkind way. Do to him
what he did to my kindhearted
daughter: rip his skin, puncture
a lung, wind a root like a wire
around his putrid throat.

11. *Victim Consciousness*

She took it
as her own
failure, you know.

The way
something absorbent
can't help but soak up
the blood of a wound,
she shouldered the guilt
of an insane culture.

12. *Graffiti / Found Poem*

In the pizza parlor
during the O. J. Simpson
murder trial, someone has carved
on the wooden wall:
No matter how hot she is
somebody somewhere
is sick of her shit.

13. *Little Narratives About Violence*

The slow flame creeps
along the weapon's
fuse. Too soon
too late to call it back
from the crisis that awaits—
the blood, the broken
bones, destroyed homes,
those images you willed
into creation that cannot
be erased and will live
to worry you forever. Like the child
you birthed but never understood,
who somehow lost her way,
and now you can't disclaim
her ties to you—those
blue-gray eyes, the slanting

cheeks, the fact—unequivocal—
that she was harbored in your body.

14. *Metaphor for Vengeance*

When the downpour dries
on the hot stones
of the cobbled plaza,
we still cannot walk there
in our naked feet.
Nor is it possible
to lie down there
in comfort
and rest.

15. *Lines for Healing*

If I hate my wounded
hand and treat it
badly, it will fester.

If I cultivate
the calm detachment
that the Gospels preach
and clean it out
and bind it up,
I will find the edges
knitting back
together, new flesh
growing, blood rerouted
to its proper channels.

I will find
my hand a hand
again.

16. *Object Lesson in the Garden #1*

I need not even
pluck it—it falls
in my palm at barest
touch of cupped hand.
Ripe tomato, warm with sun,
grown in its time
to full, red roundness,
bearing new seed within.
Now it goes forth alone—
to the table, the scrap
bowl, the compost bin,
back to the heart
of the earth's ripe mystery.

17. *Object Lesson in the Garden #2*

I set my chair beside the garden
to watch it grow exactly as I sat
beside her infant's crib, listening
to her breaths, inhaling her odors,
afraid she would perish without
my vigil. All season I maintained
my fearful watch. The sun poured down,
the rain. Despite anxiety,
my small crop grew. Now the soil
is empty of its summer fruit.
The garden meets its fate.
The dried-up stalks and desiccated
roots are what remain of what once grew.
We can't retain our beauty
or our gifts forever. We cannot keep
our children young, or safe.
The garden grows, despite us.
It bears its fruit, or not.
And then? It dies.

18. *Object Lesson in the Garden #3*

It is hard to plow
the black stalks under,
to pluck the emptied vines
and dump them on the compost heap.

It is here I failed.
I had no confidence
the seasons would return,
no solace if they didn't.

Again, I see his hands
around her neck, and there
is no excuse. But I see mine
there, too, nails gnawed down

to bloody hems of ragged flesh
on her behalf. Her mother's hands
accustomed her to endure the yoke
of others' love, and impressed on her the beauty

of ruby beads encircling a woman's throat.

19. *New Life*

In ancient cultures, parents
give their sons and daughters to the world
in rituals of dance and song when childhood's done.
They dramatize what lies beyond the breast,
papoose, and hearth. They give them what they need
to steer them through—a spear, a basket,
a silver ring for neck or nose. I must have thought
that moment would not come. Dear God,
forgive me: even now, I want it back.
And not just some, but all—the slithery body
in the baby bath, the toddler

screaming for me not to go,
the sweet sixteen in purple
peau de soie, queen of junior prom,

Instead, I have this grown-up girl
who goes to Group each Tuesday night.
She's let her hair down
from that elaborate 'do
he liked so much, and purchased
a whole new wardrobe—roomy tunics
and corduroy slacks, the burgeoning color
of crocus petals at winter's end.
She sits there with her scraped-out womb
and broken life, pushing styrofoam bits
of torn-up cups into shapes
that make a sense I still can't see.

And then she speaks:
My name is J. My husband
shot himself two months ago,
I don't know why. I'm here
because my mother grows a garden
that has brought me through.
I've sat there, crying in the rain.
I wouldn't let the melons lie
exposed in last month's frost.
The beet greens' ruffled tops
can break my heart. I crave a life
like theirs that blooms before it dies.

20. *Climacteric*

Dangling my legs from the wooden dock,
I put the petals on the water
and watch them float away.
Torn from the blossom, still

they survive for awhile, floating
in beauty, fate carrying them far
from the bush that bore them to flower.
Now, they are petals
on moving water, and the stripped
bare bloom where once they throve?
It is still alive, I say, green sap deep
in its pliant stem. Still alive,
and will bloom again, and again,
till its fullness has ended
and its time of right barrenness has come.

Portrait of the Artist as Mother

―――――――――

When an apprentice gets hurt, or complains of being tired, the workmen and peasants have this fine expression: "It is the trade entering his body." Each time that we have some pain to go through, we can say to ourselves quite truly that it is the universe, the order and beauty of the world and the obedience of creation to God that are entering our body. After that, how can we fail to bless with tenderest gratitude the Love that sends us this gift.   *—Simone Weil*

In the dank clarity of the Green Line tunnel,
we hatched our plan—to grow a creature
from those nights of love, those afternoons
of thick scents, those liquid mornings, odor
of coffee mingling with musk. Actually, he wanted
six, he said, standing there in the chill, a train
thundering up like an epiphany the two of us
verified together.

I knew then it was over, irrevocably
over, my previous life, alone and unloved, could see
how it would finally play itself out, starring him
and our creatures, the chaotic kitchen, the rumpled
beds, my wrinkled shirttails smeared with egg.
Helplessly, I tilted toward him and those sweet
images, to his mouth and his smell, toward my life
and my future, the nights we would recline, locked
and rocking in groaning love, the months my belly
would expand with our efforts, the bloody bringing forth
of two of him and one of me.

I stood for one last moment alone,
inside a cloud of grace, a pure and empty
gift of space where history released its grip.
Its bulging bag of bad memories burst open
in the doors of a train and was carried off
to a distant city I swore never to revisit.
And then I turned to his lips and his tongue,
to our hands in our gloves unbuckling each other,
calculating how quickly we could travel
back home. To anyone watching, it must have
looked like lust—two lovers emboldened
by the anonymity residing in a subway stop.
What kind of being could possibly see

a new world was being made, a universe
created? Who could have known how called
we were to what we were doing? How godlike
it was, how delicious, how holy?

FUNK

Opening the diaper, each morning
becomes the third day, when God
created the earth, late
in the afternoon, mountains
and continents firmly in place,
the waterways swinging between,
He turned His attention
to the lowlands, malodorous
and steamy, the swampy
muck of undersides mutating
already into something new,
future home of the uncivilized
creatures who will sleep in their own
dung and arise unfazed, a dazzling
smile ripping through the bars
of the crib, sunlight breaking
like tears on their slithering
bodies and their unhaired heads.

ABOVE THE BASSINETTE

This moment   this one
just here   just now   this
one moment   inhabited
by a hand reaching
through space to the top
of a head that was formed
in my body   that flourished
in there and became
this touch of tender
curls   brown and sweet
this moment   this child
    trembling
out of focus   elegiac
already   falling and
falling into the past

LOVE PIG

You, too, will love
her thighs. The fat
sweatiness of them,
the toe-curling odor.
The bracelets, the biscuits
of baby-flesh washed
in urine and milk.
The neck is next best.
Fat, too, bejeweled with dried
spit, old food, gray
gyres of tears and sweat.
If you like, I will let you
borrow her for awhile
and you can burrow
down deep in her sweet
and her sourness, her soft
and her softer. Belly up
to the buffet of her body, and grow
corpulent like us, guzzling
sweet draughts of baby breath,
gobbling mouthfuls of sticky,
tender cheek, gorging ourselves
on our own baby girl.

Ashram

To discipline
myself in this way,
to pull back
from the edge
of desire, of anger,
of the words of a poem
beginning to grow.
To lie quiet
as a creature
on the milk-stained couch
and nurse my young.
To study the shadows
the palm trees cast
on the vaulted ceiling.
To travel deeply into that,
darkly ambiguous within,
green and growing without.
To set aside the baskets
of unfolded laundry,
the blinking light
on the telephone machine,
the cut of beef thawing
in its bloody juices
on the crowded kitchen counter.

Birth Control

I, who sickened as a child
at the sluice of Sunday pudding
in my mouth, refusing
tapioca, whipped cream,
gravies, cottage cheese,
now adore the primordial
ooze of all of these,
that thick swamp soup
that brought my creatures
into being, and now, sliding
slickly from the tube
in glistening reams of sheeny gel,
prohibits life to any more
than them. And I. And he who is waiting
unclad on the unstained sheets.

I seek it in the steamy odor
of the iron pressing cotton shirts
in the heat of a summer afternoon,
in my daughter's ear, the warm pink
cone, curling inward. I seek it
in the dusty circles of the ceiling fan,
the kitchen counter with its painted shells
from Hilton Head, the creaking boards
in the bedroom floor, the coconut
cookies in the blue glass jar.
The hard brown knob of nutmeg nestled
in the silver grater and the lemon
yogurt that awaits. I seek it not
in books but in my life inscribed
in two brief words—*mother, wife*
—the life I live as mistress of an unkempt
manse, volunteer at firstborn's
school, alternate Wednesdays'
aide at youngest's nursery, billpayer,
laundress, cook, shrewd purchaser of mid-
priced minivan. I seek it
in the strophes of a life
like this, wondering what
it could be like, its narratives
drawn from the nursery and playpen,
its images besmirched with vomitus
and shit. The prayer I pray is this:

If you are here,
where are you?
If you exist,
what are you?
I beg you
to reveal yourself.
I will not judge,

I am not fancy.
My days are filled
with wiping noses
and bathing bottoms,
with boiling pots
of cheese-filled pasta
for toothless mouths
while reading Rilke,
weeping.

My life is broken
into broken pieces.
The fabric is rent.
Daily, I roll
the stone away
but all is dark
inside, unchanged.
The miracle has not
happened yet.

If you are anywhere
nearby, show me
anything at all
to prove you do exist:
a poem in a small, soiled
nightie, a lyric
in the sandbox voices
raised in woe.

Release a stanza
from the sink's hot suds
where dirty dishes glow.
Seal a message inside:
encourage me
to hold on.
Inform me
in detail
exactly how to do it.

MOVING

Old walls are new to me. Someone else's
babies were carried up this cracked brick walk,
sung over the threshold, bedded down
in the tiny orange nursery that gives off
the kitchen or in the low-roofed room upstairs
where I hope to write. Not mine
who took their first steps elsewhere
and never had their portraits posed by the short
stone fence or plucked the blossoms
from the magnolia someone planted
far too near the dank north wall.
Someone else conceived her creatures
here and struggled with the washer
in the cold dark basement. Ancient
fuses, busted lights. Other
infants haunted these nights.
Mine are quiet and sleep straight through,
uneasy in new arrangements of their furniture,
new odors, new echoes. New light on the walls.
New darkness in their hearts. And while
they sleep, I pace my newly purchased
halls choking in wallpaper I'd never choose,
dark paints that sink my spirits. Wrenched
out of context, no depth to new life
yet. On the patio, a pail is full of water
but it's frozen. My houseplants perished
on the journey here. And the first garment
I retrieve from the packed-up cartons
is a shirt with its pocket torn off, still
wearable, I guess, but capable of carrying
nothing. No money or photos, no map,
no scrap of paper with a telephone number
I need to remember. Not even a pen or a pencil
so I can write my way out of here as fast as possible.

In Praise of Single Mothers

acknowledging C. S.

That I have closed myself into my study at 8:45 P.M. on this Thursday
  evening in early October,
the paper before me, the word processor whirring for revisions, the coffee in
  its thick blue mug
fragrancing this small space beside the washing machine
which, too, whirs companionably (fifth time today).

That my chores are done, my children sleeping, and I have just begun to
  make relation with words again,
a sweet tinkly string of them tumbling lightly, back of my teeth,
about to erupt, when

The magisterial Peter Augustus, forty-five months on the planet today,
only recently weaned of his bedtime bottle,
the one with black hair and big ears
whose eyes squint suspiciously at every encounter,
it was he, intelligent and terrifying, who took the key
to the minivan and started it up, and drove it in reverse
one hundred yards down the boulevard, trying to stop it
with his hands pressed to the roof, ignorant
of steering, grim-lipped and dry-eyed, stalling out,
thank God, on the lip of a curb, placed there, obviously,
for just that reason. He, he is the one
who pushes through the bifold doors of my makeshift study
and holds forth his sippy cup with furious civility.

That I love his fierce will, his inability to compromise,
his sweet, sleek ass, the thumb in his mouth, the pale skin tightened
over the harp of his ribs. That his ear
is a spiral of unspeakable wonderment, a pinkish
cornucopia lined with hair, buttered with gold—
and down deep, last week, the black bean blocking the outer canal.

75

That I give thanks for his uniqueness in the universe
and fill his cup and chat quietly,
and pick him up in his Tiger t-shirt,
his long legs wrapped around my waist,
sucked thumb sickeningly scented,
mouth working busily at the plastic cover of his drinking cup.

That I carry him back upstairs, fifty-four pounds
straining my back, my neck tense, quadriceps pulling manfully,
and lay him down in his bed and lean into him again and again,
finally inhaling one last time, and tiptoe out, taking his beloved odor
with me on my fingertips and cheeks.

That I enclose myself once more in the laundry room/study, pondering
    briefly
the nature of discipline, remembering the self-sacrificing saints, especially
    St. Zita, lifelong servant, patroness of washerwomen, charladies,
    housekeepers, cooks, and St. Paula, widowed at thirty-three with five
    small children, renowned for her "excessive" self-mortification.
I try to be like St. Theresa of Lisieux, that exquisite
Little Flower, not mystic at all, living her simple life, finding
sainthood and sanity in the daily round of cleaning up and bringing order.

That I am not a saint, my days are marked by bitten lips and cutoff, angry
    words, my voice
rising impatiently with creatures too undeveloped to understand
those wings inside me, rising up wildly in protest of one more interruption.

That the Hail Mary calms me with its lovely images, its soothing rhythms,
    its praise for women, I say it like a mantra.

That I say three, then four, then close the study door again, shutting myself
    once more into solitude.

That I whisk my mind into a stiff froth of egg white–like consistency and
    lower myself into it as a mother and arise, rinsed into a poet, baptized
    back into words.

That something flows. The liquid of language, that liquor,
the familiar warmth, the watch melting off my arm, body
disappearing into timeless space: a sound, a rhythm, an urge
to follow. That I am flying here, and floating there, and rising
and writing . . .

Like a snake in unfamiliar territory, advancing warily, but slowly gaining in
      confidence
and volume, a sound is born.

That she wails, she wails, she wails.

That I arise and go to her automatically.

That this one, at least, is quiet, can't talk, and fits
into one arm's crook, tightly bound inside a blanket,
I am thankful, and so race to retrieve her.
That the breasts turn on in concert, predictable
as a percolator on automatic timer, the milk
warming and rising, the breasts suddenly stuffed
sausages, uncomfortable and embarrassing.

That I love my milk, my mother's milk,
thin and sweet, yellow and oily,
and she does, too, wailing now
at a volume that threatens the sleep of the others.
That I lift her up hastily with one hand,
the other ripping at the clever closing
of the nursing bra, the pads already soaked through
and dropping to the floor with a sodden thunk.

That she clamps on with a moan, and wrenches
my nipple with her toothless, bone-hard gums,
reproaching me for my tardiness.
That my last line written downstairs—was it
a line? an entire line? maybe just an image, fleeting but brilliant—
that last hard-earned line (or whatever it was) must still be blinking behind

the cursor, mustn't it? Unless
I forgot to save it again.

That the milk is flowing now,
the endorphins surging through my head and torso,
even the pads of my feet feel good,
we tumble backward, she and I, onto the futon
her father and I conceived her on.
That I think about that for awhile, body swelling
and pulsing in various locations.
Whatever that line was, I can't
worry about it now, the machine
has it, surely. Entirely, I trust
technology, though I'm milk
and heat, white softnesses and the smell
her mouth emits opening to switch
to the other tit.

That we sink into it, whatever we are,
whatever I am, nursing mother, postpartum
poet-on-pause, being suckled and holding,
sucking and being held, mother and daughter,
her mouth on my breast, my hand on her head,
our eyes on each other's.

That she drains me and I do not
even care, holding her there
in the time-stopped, milky darkness.

That the two of us are lovers.

That I love her.

That I love her more,
much more, than poetry.

That the cursor blinks blankly
at the end of an empty line.

In My Office at Bennington

Mornings, I sit by the open window
in the red barn, reading poems
and quietly thinking. Coffee idles
in a cracked blue mug, and bees burst
in and out of the unscreened window.
At last, a poem seems possible
again—brain knitting a scarf
of thought, purling it into words.
Metaphors emerge after long seclusion—
a green crocus, crusted with dirt, thrusts
through the rotten fabric of an ailing lawn
late in February. The season is almost
over, or it's not, in fact, begun.

But then I hear the voices of my children
returning from a meal, hiking up the hill
from camp. Or the plastic wheels of Janey's
carriage clattering in gravel.
The cheerful firstborn's off-key whistle,
airy through the gap in new front teeth

and I'm paper torn in half,

the poem that didn't work,
the wrong words, sour sounds,
ruptured rhythms, the confusion
as to what was meant, what I actually
desired besides those three small faces
raised to my open window, calling
my name over and over, *Mama?*

The Madness

The words
or their bodies

Is it I
or them

In the end
who will win?

FAREWELL TO THE MAIDEN

for Mary Deshazer

If the body's a text,
this must be the end
of my Bildungsroman.
Heavy with content, my plot
propelled by fate and necessity,
youth is a dream of earlier
chapters. Only flashbacks remain
to the creamy thighs,
unlined neck, the taut
still pond of my maiden's stomach.
Whose subject am I now
but my own? Corners bent, pages
wrinkled, my text is a mess
but original. Once, I wished
to be a verse of gorgeous sinuosity,
a lyric poem, some tightly belted
perfect sonnet or deftly figured
villanelle. Not to be. Bildungsroman
called me in its loud, coarse voice.
That big, fat book that finds its form
simply by following a life.

DISJUNCTION

On my knees in my office,
leaning over the metal can
of waste, I squeeze my breasts
to express the milk that's accrued
in my graduate seminar on postmodern
poetry. Six hours since the last feed
and only eight weeks postpartum,
the pressure's enough to kill a cow.
Talking head reduced by hormones
to a pitiful creature on bended knee
weeping and milking her own hot tits.
It's thin and blue, this milk intended
for my daughter's mouth. Instead,
it's spurting coolly on my ink-stained hands,
dribbling in a painful start, then flowing
unencumbered on the paper detritus
of my chosen work—the dean's agenda
for the faculty meeting, a debatable
policy on sexual harassment,
the first draft of some idiot's
poem on fraternity love: unprotected
rutting on a bed of crushed empties.
        —Life is so unutterably
weird, isn't it? Organizing my thoughts
on the cultural disjunctions of the end
of the century and how they break their way into
our literature and art, and how bizarre
is the era that finds me here
wastefully wringing the milk from my breasts
in the same office where I scheme to procure
permanent tenure.

POEM FOR ROBIN

When your mother told me
of your weeping, of your lying
in her bed, of your head sharing the pillow
with hers, of your three days
of tears when she returned home
after the mastectomy, inside, I
wept, keeping my eyes clear and stone
hard for my friend, your mother.

You're still too young to know
what you've done. You think it's merely
one more lesson in growing up—more pain, more loss.
You've come to see all bets are off.
But lying there on that pillow, weeping,
you became her infant again, called back
to those days when you had just emerged
from her bleeding body. That was when
you first gave shape to life for her, when she lifted you
to her breast, now lost, and gave you
life. And now you give it back, lying there
in your grown-up body, weeping, calling her name
over and over, tying her to this life, this love,
this daughter who will not let her go.

NECKS

Because he looked undamaged
when they raised him
from the water, because
his mother failed to see him fall,
I still rise each night to ascertain
my sleeping children live, to touch
their stilled and silent
bodies, to press my face
against their throats, inhaling
odors that are theirs alone.
The pulse lives in the neck, as does
the breath, and that is why, I guess,
I go there to dialogue with God, and avail myself
of the bony cup the collarbone provides
for my teary alms of gratitude and fear.

Catholic

How I miss the lurid
symphonic sound of two bodies
mating in the dark. Now, it's a littler
tune, a brew of bodies actual
and about-to-be. The cacophonous
sounds—coughs and wails, the creaking
springs of aging cribs—of those
who've arrived already furnish
our imaginations with innovative ways
to do it speedily in silence.

And those who do not
make it, those who clamor
to *be* through our sweating,
yearning bodies, but fail,
I wipe away reverently, or let
dry, encrusted, on my inner
thighs. There, I celebrate
the force of life each time
their funky scent ascends
from the altar of my body.

GODLESS

Their daughter became very ill.
She who loved, it seemed,
so much this life—her capacity
for seeing it in captivating
moments of still life and broken-off
bits of literature. She
of the shatteringly perfect birthday
gifts—the full-headed peony
in the cut-glass vase, the green leaves
knotted in the bronze-colored scarf.
Bizarrely, it was *she,* not some
dullard poking at a calculator,
nor some idiot gunning down
neighbors in an alley. No.
It was she of the magical
insights and the flair for living
whose body was chosen to fail.

The altar was a secular place.
No word of prayer would cross
their lips. No cry for help.
For two years, she labored there
to survive, then die. And now
she is gone—her body a horrible
object they burned to a crisp.
On the mantel, it waits in a gorgeous jar
for just that place, that color
of light, the right trembling of air
in the sycamore trees. *Then,* they think,
they will find her again
when they dump her out as now
they cannot, wandering the woods,

calling her name in their aching heads,
wondering where it is her *is-ness*
has fled, and why it seems so stubbornly
as if she never existed.

AFTER READING REZNIKOFF

When I think of those mothers giving up
their children at the gates of the camps,
or choosing one over the other, or accompanying
their youngsters to the showers of gas,
when I think of that wrenching, that
wailing, the force of those feelings,
the terrible potency, the fear breaking
their bodies in sweat and hives,
the vomiting and shitting, the mindless
lunging for their infants and toddlers,
their sons and their daughters, when I think of
that universe of last images, the eyes, the unspeakable
eyes of mothers comprehending, the backs
of the children waddling away, being led
away, being pulled away, recalcitrant curls,
fallen hems, toys dropped on the gravel paths,
the little waves, the dipped heads, the incessant
weeping, when I think of the bleeding wombs
of dying mothers, pleading mothers, the bellies
of mothers with unborn babies, the breasts bursting
with unsucked milk, when I think of the various
ways the weather must have been—the cold
crunch of snow, the flowery delight of early spring
—when I think of the camps and the deaths of the Jews,
the millions of Jews, I think of the mothers,
the bodies of mothers, their bodies bearing
their children to death, I think of the noise
of transport trains, the terror of trains,
the engines cooling into inert steel,
the clatter and steam, the scenes enacted
in the railroad yards, and the trains remind me
to think of the men, at last I remember
those armies of men, their greatcoats and weapons,

no children inhabiting their rational bodies, the mystery
of murder, the bodies of the women so alive
with emotion, the bodies of the men so dead
to it all, I think not of God, desperately I try
to not think of God, my good, great God, neither
woman nor man, circling above in heartbroken panic,
the beating of wings, the cacophonous
suffering, the pungent cloud rising
of dark, dark feeling that silenced even Him.

INSCRUTABLE

The face seen
for the first time
screwed up and wetted
with the juices of my body,
the hair swirled down
into flattened, greasy
curls, the mathematical
perfection of the four
extremities, the primitive
muscles of the mouth and jaw
already shaped around sucking,
and just the goddamn mystery
of it all—why there is
anything, anything at all
rather than nothing emerging
from the bloody hole
in my opened body, why
anything like this face, this
body that slithers from mine,
this call to claim it
undimmed after eons, irresistible
and thrilling as sexual
longing, why God leaning over
the paradise He made, why
splitting Himself to become
the first creature,
why in love with the world
for the rest of eternity,
alone no longer, inviolate
          no more. Why God? Why love? Why
this infant sucking me and why
me—desperate and hemorrhaging

on the surgical table—why
weeping with gratitude
to be this way,
exactly this way, instead of some other?

PRAYER FOR MY CHILDREN

I regret nothing.
My cruelties, my betrayals
of others I once thought
I loved. All the unlived
years, the unwritten
poems, the wasted nights
spent weeping and drinking.

No, I regret nothing
because what I've lived
has led me here, to this room
with its marvelous riches,
its simple wealth—
these three heads shining
beneath the Japanese lamp, laboring
over crayons and paper.
These three who love me
exactly as I am, precisely
at the center of my ill-built being.
Who rear up eagerly when I enter,
and fall down weeping when I leave.
Whose eyes are my eyes.
Hair, my hair.
Whose bodies I cover
with kisses and blankets.
Whose first meal was my own body.
Whose last, please God, I will not live
to serve, or share.

Acknowledgments

Philip Levine and Diann Blakely read this book in manuscript and offered valuable suggestions and comments. I am grateful to them.

The College of Arts and Sciences at Louisiana State University funded a summer research fellowship for work on "The Testimony of Simone Weil." It was a source of great support early in the work on this book.

I have been privileged to serve as poet in residence at Duke University Medical Center and Vanderbilt University Medical Center. Both of these arts programs were enormously supportive of my writing, the demands of mothering, and my chaotic personal style. I thank Janice Palmer and Bunny Burson for their help and forbearance, Jenny Lewis for her "technical support," and the Osler Literary Roundtable at Duke for introducing me to a new community of readers and writers.

Many of my women friends have helped me write these poems and put this book together. I can't thank them all, but must single out Shelley Reisman Paine, girlfriend and neighbor *extraordinaire,* Cedar Koons, and some of my former colleagues in the writing seminars at Bennington College: Jill McCorkle, Susan Cheever, and Betsy Cox—marvelous examples of equanimity in mothering and writing. Thank you all.

Finally, I thank my husband and my children for everything they have given me, which, in fact, is everything that matters at all.

Notes

The Testimony of Simone Weil

The enormous complexity of Simone Weil's thought and personality can only be hinted at, grasped after, in a poem like this. Obviously, I see a strong connection between her consciousness and the visual images produced by Eugène Atget. What follows is an idiosyncratic chronology of Weil's life, an annotation to the various events that serve as occasions in the poem. Her own works include very little personal material. For that, consult the various biographies, including *Simone Weil: A Life,* by Simone Petrement (New York: Pantheon, 1976), and *Simone Weil: A Modern Pilgrimage,* by Robert Coles (Reading, MA: Addison-Wesley, 1987).

1909: S. W. born in Paris to upper-middle-class Jewish (nonpracticing) parents, Dr. Bernard Weil and Selma Weil. Her only sibling is her older brother, André (b. 1906), who displays early brilliance in mathematics. S. W. and André are close, though S. W. is convinced of her intellectual inferiority to her brother, and often wishes she had been born a boy (Simon).

1914: Dr. Weil is called up when World War I begins. The family embarks on a nomadic period of several years as Mme. Weil, with her children, follows her husband to each of his postings. S. W. educated by correspondence lessons. This is also the year she first exhibits anorexic tendencies, refusing, at age five, to eat sugar because it is not available to the French troops on the front. Supposedly, a Weil domestic did suggest that she was a saint.

1921: Onset, at age twelve, of the migraine headaches that will suffer without relief throughout her life.

1925: Takes her *baccalauréat* in philosophy from Lycée Victor Duruy. Enters the Lycée Henri IV, where she studies under the philosopher Émile Auguste Chartier (1868–1952), who is known under his pen name, Alain. It is he who nicknames her "Martian," calling attention to her pronounced devaluing of her femininity and the ferocious intensity that she displays in her intellectual pursuits. "It is incontestable that the void which we grasp with the pincers of contradiction is from on high, for we grasp it the better the more we sharpen our natural faculties of intelligence, will and love. The void which is from below is that into which we fall when we allow our natural faculties to become atrophied."

1928: Enters the École Normale Supérieure, placing first in the entrance exams, followed by Simone de Beauvoir. It is here that she becomes acquainted with leftist politics and demonstrates an extreme sympathy for workers and their conditions. "As for the spirit of poverty, I do not remember any moment when it was not in me."

1931: Graduates, having completed a thesis, "Science and Perception in Descartes," and having performed brilliantly on her exit examinations. Goes to work teaching philosophy at a girls' school near Lyons. For the first part of the decade, her writings focus on social problems and class issues.

1932: After involving herself in public demonstrations on behalf of the unemployed, she is transferred to another position in Auxerre. Again, there are problems, and ultimately her position is eliminated.

1934: On leave from teaching, she undertakes work in the three factories named in the poem. "There I received forever the mark of a slave."

1936: In the spring, she investigates the lives of rural farmworkers by laboring on a family farm in Cher. In August, she travels to Barcelona to join the Republican front. She hooks up with an anarchist trade union and, in one of their field camps, has the accident with the pot of hot oil. Evacuates herself to hospital in Sitges.

1937: Declining health. Sick leave from teaching extended. In the spring, in Assisi, she is moved for the first time to kneel and pray. "Something stronger than I was compelled me for the first time in my life to go down on my knees."

1938: At Easter, at the Benedictine abbey in Solesmes, she experiences a visitation from Christ. "Christ himself came down and took possession of me." It is here that she first reads the English metaphysical poets and becomes particularly attached to George Herbert's "Love," which she begins thereafter to recite to herself during her bouts with migraines. "I learned it by heart. Often at the culminating point of a violent headache, I make myself say it over, concentrating all my attention upon it and clinging with all my soul to the tenderness it enshrines." Writing begins to show her extreme religiosity and her particular interest in Catholicism.

1940–42: Living in Vichy and Marseilles. Dismissed from her teaching position under the Vichy laws. Her writings are dominated by contemplation of the supernatural and the mystical. Meets her spiritual directors in her continuing journey toward Catholicism—the Dominican monk, Father J.-M. Perrin, and the Catholic writer, Gustave Thibon. Leaves her notebooks (to become *Gravity and Grace*) with Thibon when she sails with her parents to the United States.

1942–43: In New York, she attends mass every day. In November, she sails alone to England and eventually finds work with the Free French resistance movement in London. Writes *The Need for Roots*. Becomes increasingly anorexic, which she attributes to solidarity with the occupied French. Her health deteriorates rapidly. Diagnosed with tuberculosis, she refuses treatment and food. Though visited by a Catholic priest, she continues to reject baptism. "I have always remained at this exact point, on the threshold of the Church, without moving, quite still." Admitted to a sanatorium in Ashford, Kent, she dies on August 24, 1943, of pulmonary tuberculosis and self-starvation. "We have to pass through death. We have to be killed—to endure the weight of the world. When the universe is weighing upon the back of a human creature, what is there to be surprised if it hurts him?"

Quotations are from "Spiritual Autobiography," in *The Simone Weil Reader,* and *Gravity and Grace,* by S. W.

In the Marvelous Dimension

The San Francisco earthquake occurred on October 17, 1989, at 5:04 P.M. It measured 6.9 on the Richter scale and lasted about fifteen seconds. In those few moments, seven billion dollars' worth of damage was caused in the Bay Area. The upper deck of the Nimitz Freeway in Oakland collapsed, crushing vehicles and trapping their occupants, killing forty-two people.

Portrait of the Artist as Mother

Genesis 1:28: "God blessed them, saying: 'Be fertile and multiply; fill the earth and subdue it. Have dominion over the fish of the sea, the birds of the air, and all the living things that move on earth.'" From *The New American Bible* (New York: Catholic Book Publishing Company, 1986), 4–5.

In Praise of Single Mothers: I'm tipping my hat, of course, to the eighteenth-century English poet Christopher Smart, author of "Jubilato Agno" (more familiarly known as "For I Will Consider My Cat Jeoffrey"), a rapturous poem of pet-love, written while Smart was confined for insanity.

After Reading Reznikoff: *Holocaust*, by Charles Reznikoff (Santa Barbara: Black Sparrow Press, 1975, 1977), is based on the transcripts of the Nuremberg and Eichmann trials.

Works Cited

p. 1   "God can . . ." and "It is when . . ." are from *Gravity and Grace,* by Simone Weil (London, New York: Ark Paperbacks, 1987), 99, 102.

"To love truth . . ." is from *The Notebooks of Simone Weil,* I (London: Routledge & Kegan Paul, 1976), 160–61.

"As Atget grew . . ." is from *The Work of Atget,* I, text by John Szarkowski (New York: Museum of Modern Art, 1981), 22–23.

"Other people . . ." is from *Masters of Photography: Eugène Atget,* text by Gerry Badger (London: Macdonald and Company, 1985), unpaginated.

p. 9   Photo reference is *Marchand de vin, rue Boyer,* reproduced in *Atget's Seven Albums,* by Molly Nesbitt (New Haven: Yale University Press, 1992), 376.

p. 10   "totally reduced . . ." is from *The Notebooks of Simone Weil,* I, 157.

p. 11   Photo reference is *Versailles Parc du Château Amphithéâtre de Verdun,* reproduced in *Masters of Photography.*

pp. 14–15 A selection of the prostitute photos can be found in *The Work of Atget,* IV (1985).

p. 18   Atget's interiors are reproduced in *Atget's Seven Albums,* 338–48.

p. 20   Photo reference is *Entrée des jardins,* reproduced in *The Work of Atget,* IV, 57.

p. 21   "Decreation . . ." and "We must become . . ." are from *Gravity and Grace*, 28, 32.

pp. 21–22   Photo reference is *Tuileries—Côte de la Concorde*, reproduced in *Atget's Seven Albums*, 70.

p. 23   *Les chiffonniers* are reproduced in *Atget's Seven Albums*, 398–412.

pp. 23–24   Photo reference is *Coin de la rue de Bievre*, reproduced in *Atget's Seven Albums*, 74.

p. 27   "Affliction is . . ." is from "The Love of God and Affliction" in *Waiting for God*, by Simone Weil (New York: Harper and Row/Perennial Library, 1973), 131.

p. 45   "On the whole . . ." is from "Sketch of Contemporary Social Life," in *The Simone Weil Reader*, edited by George Panichas (New York: David McKay Company, 1977), 452.

p. 63   "When an apprentice . . ." is from *Waiting for God*, 131.